The Renovated Jewish State

Yehiel Tzur

VANTAGE PRESS
New York

To the near coming of the Messiah, the salvation of Israel, and the greatness and glory of the Jewish state as it was meant to be and as it shall be.

FIRST EDITION

Copyright © 1993 by Yehiel Tzur

Published by Vantage Press, Inc.
516 West 34th Street, New York, New York 10001

Manufactured in the United States of America
ISBN: 0-533-10685-0

Library of Congress Catalog Card No.: 93-93925

0 9 8 7 6 5 4 3 2 1

Contents

Introduction

The subject of this manifesto might be summarized in one simple word—**CHANGE!**

The change I am advocating making is related to the way we have conceived and later executed an ancient idea, none other than the establishment of the Jewish state of Israel.

Since that exalted day in 1948, many Jews have engaged in a debate as to whether the idea's realization within the framework to which it was molded over the last fifty years has indeed come to serve the purpose for which the idea was promulgated in the first place.

My answer to that would be simply **NO!**

To my observation, this idea was adapted in a direction unparallel to the course it was destined to take. Yet I would not label it unequivocally a mistake. The reason is that I cannot portray a political-economical composition different from that which was adopted by the founding fathers and which was able to realize the idea, considering the means they had at their disposal and the mentalities they were working with, in the face of the socio-economic situation that existed in their native lands. On the other hand, their adherence to an ideology that has proven through the years to be ineffective and dissimilar to the changing world reality is nothing less than a clear mistake.

In 1896 the prophecy by the name of *The Jewish State,* by Dr. Theodor Herzl, was published. In it he wrote: "We will learn from the historical mistakes of others as well as from our own. For we are a modern people who wish to be the most modern amongst the nations."

No one will dare to doubt the unexhausted devotion and efforts of Jewish pioneers who contributed to the lofty achievements of the young Jewish nation and advanced her into the front rank of nations. But will there rise a man who will refuse to admit the economic dependence of the pioneering enterprise upon the donations of foreigners and even the strange generosity of Gentile nations? Will there rise a man who can assure us that these donations and generosities will continue forever?

God forbid **NO!**

A search for such an assurance would be a sin and an invitation for disaster dealt us by anti-Semites and God's fury. However, to my deep concern, truth shows that this misconception is the estate of many in Israel; in other words, it is another historical mistake we stand to repeat in spite of Herzl's wise and simple suggestion, which still waits to be applied by us.

Economic independence was an impossible aim to achieve together with our political independence because no state in history was born without the assistance of others. Fifty years since and we still aspire to economic independence. It strikes me why we have not succeeded so far. It strikes me why a people who are known for their intellectual capacities, shrewd thinking, and undiminished contributions to the prosperity of nations and the Industrial Revolution could not bring prosperity to their own homeland.

There will be those who would reply with the old excuse that fifty years are not enough for such an ambitious aim. Such an answer is acceptable only if we were living in an existing Jewish state in a previous century.

The end of the twentieth century and the beginning of the twenty-first is a reality in which technology, modernization, liberty, and ideas are changing directions quickly and without pause; a reality in which changes themselves, whether revolutionary or not, are the only means of individuals as well as of nations to acclimate and survive. This understanding, as I indicated earlier, is the subject of this manifesto; change is necessary to save and uphold the Zionist idea.

It would be appropriate to point out right now that I am not imagining a thing, for the facts are standing naked before us. Likewise, I am not inventing the methods to fix them. For the most part, I am gathering and embracing ideas that already exist and are self-evident; I am merely explaining them in language that is accessible to everyone. I would add that it is not my intention to deal with details and technicalities. What I will present are general elements. The missing blanks will be left to be filled in by the imagination of the rational reader to whom I apply.

I am aware of the outrage that will arise after, perhaps even before, I finish. I know that it will be orchestrated both by anti-Semites and self-hating Jews. They will accuse me of being a revolutionary, a fascist, an inciter, and even a daydreamer when, in fact, my only demand is for renovation and inauguration. Nevertheless, I am not alone in the act. Many Jews of my generation stand for the same opinions I do; their cries echo all over the country and into the Knesset, Israel's legislature, which is still wrapped in the stubbornness and narrowmindedness of fainthearted old Jewish politicians.

I am not hesitating to reveal that, according to my instinct, change is inevitable and there is no alternative. Those who seek easy compromises or ask to maintain the status quo are asking for national suicide and the destruction of the state of Israel. Thus "To be or not to be?" is, indeed, the question!

My exclusive belief is that Israel, with appropriate political, social, and economic changes and an altered vision, will succeed in realizing that same ancient idea in its entirety, meaning that the salvation of our people will come together with the greatness and glory of our homeland. Then, of course, peace will prevail between us and our enemies. Thus let it be clear before our eyes from the beginning! Neither war nor peace can stand in the way of this renovation and realization; only the indifference, ignorance, and foolishness of the Jewish people are liable to be obstacles.

As for the question of when this change will occur, I can answer with certainty, by sentiment as much as by reason, that it will occur within my lifetime. Therefore, I hope that, in addition to the task that I have undertaken in publishing this manifesto, I will be able to contribute to this change with more tangible deeds. However, our destiny cannot be fulfilled by my sentiment, beliefs, and reason alone. Many Jews will have to join in the act, along with those harnessed to it already. They will have to possess superior freshness, determination, and readiness to sacrifice of themselves, just as the pioneers did in their time.

In short, "To the Jews who will, it is not a fairy tale. They will have their state, and they will deserve it."

Part I

Within the Wind of Change

Chapter One
In the Labyrinth of the Status Quo

Nineteen seventy-seven was a year of unprecedented significance in Israel's young and turbulent history. It was a year of change, and without mentioning where this change led us to, let me emphasize that it was a change after all. On the one hand, it was a change that symbolized the maturity of Israeli voters; on the other, it was a change in the economic perception of the Israeli society.

As implied, I am referring to the Likud's rise into power in Israel, a party classified as the conservative right and whose economic ideals are liberal.

That same year, the Likud received a mandate from the people to change an economic reality that was created in undiminished measure as a result of thirty years of continuous socialist regime; only that history, according to my reading, has shown that the only change the Likud succeeded in making in that regard was in increasing the unfolding magnitude of that same reality.

I am not coming herewith to support one party or another, because I do not belong to any of them; in fact, I hold them all in contempt. However, I come here to evoke the Jewish public in Israel before a sinister conspiracy of Israeli socialism, to pass the responsibility for its economic neglect on to the Likud party, which deserves esteem for its effort to introduce economic reforms into the Israeli market, even though it has failed due to powerful and well-organized socialist groups.

It would be appropriate to specify and explain that during the years in which the Labor party was in power an exclusive cooperation existed between it and the Histadrot, the general workers' union organization, due to which a relative economic stability was maintained. Back then, for example, we did not see the Histadrot persistently pursuing and threatening the Labor government for salary raises equal to the market's increasing prices. It certainly went satisfied for much less than that; otherwise inflation would have run wild from 1948. On the other hand, when Labor's rival, and therefore the rival of Histadrot, too, ascended to power, the two professed to be fighters for workers' rights while their real attention was to cause the Likud government to fail. Indeed, the growing weight of demands by the Histadrot, the Labor party, and other socialist bodies compelled the new government to cause indirectly inflation of hundreds of percents.

The events that have occurred since that fateful year until today are well known. I know that no one will object to my saying that the Israeli economy has become more and more dependent upon foreign aid during that period of time and, as a result, has become more vulnerable and exposed to outside pressure and maneuvers. Moreover, what affected our country's negative images most was an impasse in the political system of our nation, which paralyzed the government's mechanism, preventing it from taking clear and effective action.

The Political System

Since I considered myself mature enough to engage in political thinking, I have noticed that the political establishment in Israel has become obsolete and in several aspects undemocratic. While other parliamentary democracies in Europe seem to provide stability for their countries, the Israeli version of that same system has proven to be an obstacle to the unity and leadership of our people. It has created a government that deals with subordinate issues; a government that shows indifference and a lack of conduct, guidance, and capability to face the fate of matters. It substituted the words *compulsion* and *blackmail* for *coalition* and *consensus*. It forced prime ministers to be swept away from their original ideals for which they were elected and to be subject to pressures and influences by ministers in their government, whom they did not choose or appoint.

In fact, only in such a spoiled system can a government minister, intentionally and publicly, object or contradict the prime minister without fear of being discharged; only in such a corrupt system can a government minister who is suspected of criminal activities continue to serve in his post, for otherwise he would be liable to break the coalition government and therefore bring about its fall; only in such a greedy and disloyal system can a political candidate be bought with big contributions from abroad; only in such a confused and uncoordinated system can precious weeks and sometimes months pass from the moment of election to the moment a prime minister is announced and a cabinet selected; and only in such a contemptible and pitiful system can the prime minister be seen humiliated while wooing the support of minority parties in his government. Since the minority is literally surrendered with equal power to the majority, it is capable of dictating and holding hostage government's policies, which results in binding Israel's democracy to the altar. Finally, only in a feudal system such as ours is it possible that members of the Knesset are mostly residents of Tel Aviv or Jerusalem or associated with the army, Histadrot, or kibbutzim, while other parts and sectors of the country and Jewish population are literally left unrepresented.

To summarize, our politicians have already lost the public trust in them, and we have lost our faith in the system they represent. Hence if we were to judge them and their system by what they produce, then the ruling obviously would be that they have produced the worst results starting way back, and therefore the imperative to change them and change them fast comes in.

The Economic System

The vision of the founding fathers was of a self-sufficient economy that would provide the Jews of the land of Israel with their most basic needs and perhaps little more than that—in other words, an economy that would provide the sons of the nation with comfort, dignity, social equality, and security.

The present, on the other hand, shows this vision to be in contrast with Israel's economic reality. Today Israel is a state that owes debts to other countries totalling approximately $40 billion. To make that a more imaginable amount, I would say that each man, woman, and child in Israel owes $8,000 to nations abroad, while there is no guaranty on the horizon that this amount will cease to rise. Israel is a state whose currency is unstable and which has no international standing whatsoever and where inflation has become part of the culture and luxury imports a social prestige when, ironically, the squandering mentality of the Israeli society is rooted in the phenomenon of taking for granted contributions and loans from abroad.

As of today, Israel is immersed in an unemployment crisis that is liable to deteriorate to a level similar to that of the great Depression which commanded the Western world during the 1930s. Aside from the reasons of failing leadership and management, it is very likely that this crisis resulted from lack of ambition and motivation of Israelis to work. Apparently, because of an economic tradition that stands for establishing employment springs by government initiative and subsidies, even when there is no hope at all for profitability or any other economic benefit whatsoever, at the same time it guarantees permanence or compensation in case of discharge.

Worse than that, the Histadrot establishment, which professed to see to the vision's realization, had corrupted the foundation upon which it was created and, together with that vision, gone bankrupt. Nevertheless, it still controls more than 70 percent of the labor force and up to one-third of Israeli market's means and serves simultaneously as labor union, employer, and arbitrator all together.

Such power and contrast of interests damage the democratic character of the state, for it allows certain individuals in the Histadrot, who can, as it is, be part of the political establishment, to lock out the entire Israeli economy.

Taxes are the reason for most of our frustrations and the economic recession. Combining all the taxes, duties, tolls, impositions, etc., that are customary in Israel will crown us in the world's book of records. An exact representation of Israeli taxes would make foreign investors feel sick and run for their lives.

The complex and many-branched tax code has already done its share to impoverish the middle class and fade the dream of social equality. According to statistics about poverty in Israel in 1991 that were released by the Institution for Social Security, 562,000 Israelis lived in poverty that year, meaning that more than 11 percent of the Israeli population was impoverished, and that Jews who worked harder than ever to see the benefits of their labor had to pay up to 60 percent of their earnings in taxes.

Many taxes are absolutely absurd and serve no reasonable purpose; they put our patience, conciliation, and consciousness to the test. Politicians use them to restrain our standard of living, while they pamper themselves with all kinds of benefits and expenditures that help them remain isolated in an unrealistic, hypocritical obsession and world, in hopes of breaking commitments they promised to get elected. In their service is the income tax collection agency, which stereotypes every taxpayer as a cheater and operates in an intimidating manner, as if it was a secret police. More sinister and devious than that is the fact that they allow the banks to bribe and corrupt us with "overdrafts," which we spend on luxuries. It is not credit whatsoever, but their fraud and our greed.

In short, we must uproot this impurity within us, start from a new beginning, and revive the vision of our founding fathers.

The Social Dimension

Naturally, when a person fails, errs, or falls victim to inevitable circumstances, he is pursued by his conscience and possessed by hopelessness. He is so hesitant and confused that already he forgets his achievements and good deeds; the fear that he will repeat this nature is what drives him to do uninterrupted soul-searching and forces him to improve his shortcomings.

If all of us will follow this conduct, it would benefit us to leave our glory to the judgment of God and our disgrace to our own scrutiny.

Individualism has hit Israel with extremism, especially now, in a period when she must be united more than ever. We have become more introverted and less concerned for one another; more materialistic and accepting less responsibility for our deeds; more neglectful and feeling less guilty for it; wanting to receive more, yet willing to sacrifice much less.

The blame for it is inflicted in our hands, and as for the

loopholes that allowed such phenomena to possess us, we ought to look for them in our family fortresses.

The Jewish family is the nucleus of the nation as a whole; thus anything that undermines the foundation upon which it stands will destabilize the cohesion of the people. To my regret, during the last twenty years we have seen negative trends in this sacred institution, in the sense of domestic violence, sexual abuse, financial despair, and eventually divorce.

If once the word *divorce* was imputed with stigma, today's young generation of Israeli Jews have grown up with that concept without making a big deal out of it. It is almost difficult not to notice children of divorced parents; we can find them in every class and kindergarten. It is hard to ignore the difficulties that might develop during their childhood and affect them for the rest of their lives, not to mention the influence they might have upon our way of life and thinking as a nation.

For the last twenty years there has been a 120 percent increase in the divorce rate, as opposed to a 4 percent decrease in the number of marriages in Israel. In 1974, for example, 32,400 couples got married and 2,800 got divorced. In 1990, on the other hand, 31,300 couples got married while 6,300 got divorced.

These facts reflect, in great portions, the crumbling of social and traditional values, and where can we find the more complete reflection of that if not in Israel's parliament, the Knesset? There we see our so-called representatives engage in ugly confrontations; they tend to exceed acceptable behavior, speak profane language, and defame one another to protect their own status, integrity, and honor. In fact, they desecrate therein the invaluable service they were chosen to give and, as well, the moral standard that people like them must show. But more outrageous than that is the fact that several Knesset members allow themselves to act above the law and thus present the public with the image of deceptive and corrupt politicians.

Indeed, lawlessness and irresponsibility of key government officials and public servants have guided many of us into dark ways. Crime in our country is growing every year, whether it is theft, fraud, tax evasion, drug abuse, or even rape and murder.

Here is where our shame lies. Only we can decide what to do about it.

The Educational System

The educational system in Israel used to be one of the best in the world. Today it is on the verge of collapse. My memories of the schools I studied in are of crowded classes, violence among students, vandalism, disrespect to underpaid teachers, drugs, knives, and, to my deep regret, a high rate of failures.

Personally, I was an excellent student, but I remember my friends who were not as fortunate as I needing to supplement their education with private lessons, to encompass things they could not understand or had difficulties with in school. Their parents had to pay a heavy price to fill in what the schools were supposed to provide in the first place.

I did not have the opportunity to experience the intimidating Bagrot examinations (comprehensive high school final examinations), because my family and I left Israel when I graduated from ninth grade, as I shall explain later. But from what I was able to observe during the time I was in high school I came to the conclusion that these examinations are not the key to higher education in Israel, but rather an obstacle. The results of these examinations became through the years a matter of prestige and competition among high school principals. They serve as a tool in the hands of key officials on the boards of education to promote personal interests, while relentlessly cutting the opportunities of young students who still have their talents hidden or developing.

The obsession of teachers with making as many students as possible pass the Bagrot examinations creates discrimination between students and results in abandoning those who seem to face heavy odds in passing these difficult examinations. This is a counterproductive policy that eventually compels young Israelis to leave their country in order to study in universities abroad, which are much less difficult to gain admission to. Unfortunately, not a few of them decide not to come back to Israel after their graduation. This testing policy is one that must be reformed, and in the light of the technological and economic challenges that will confront Israel with the beginning of the twenty-first century, Israelis must commit themselves to providing free access to higher education for all who desire such, so that we as a nation will be able to face world's competition and perhaps be in the lead.

Neglect of the Emigration Problem

We rejoiced over the scenes of Russian and Ethiopian Jews coming down in great numbers from an El-Al jet and walking for the first time in their lives in the holy land of Israel, anxious to become an integral part of the nation. The irony is that at the same time, in one of the planes awaiting for departure from Ben-Gurion airport, a terrible tragedy unfolded that undermined the perception above, a tragedy that affected me personally, the emigration of Jews from Israel.

Unlike during the cold war era, Jews who live in former

communist countries enjoy freedoms they never knew before. Today they have the opportunity of thinking twice as to whether to immigrate to Israel or other countries. To my regret, Zionism is not a convincing factor in their decision anymore. However, most of those who eventually immigrate to Israel are forced to do so for two basic reasons:

A) They are so impoverished that they cannot afford doing without the free transportation and governmental aid the state of Israel will provide them with, unlike any other country on earth.
B) They are devoid of any other alternative because of clandestine agreements between the state of Israel and their native lands.

In truth, contrary to the propaganda of our country, increase in population due to immigration to Israel is much smaller than we believe, and before the present wave of immigration it even was at certain times not a factor. The reason? Together with immigration to Israel there is a mass emigration from the country, known by its popular name: Yerida.

As of today, close to 1 million Israelis reside outside of Israel, mostly in the United States and Canada. They are Jews who reluctantly abandoned their country's borders in the face of reality, and in hope of returning one day. However, many of them never will realize their hope but eventually will accept permanent exile.

In 1989, for example, the year in which my family and I immigrated to the United States, 2,192 Israelis returned home while 17,000 emigrated from it. Since then, the statistics have not changed to encourage us.

The reason my family left Israel, quite frankly, was not economic or any sort of reason that could be acceptable to the patriots among us. The reason was simply in order to facilitate a family reunion with my mother's brother, who immigrated to the United States from the Soviet Union in 1978, and my father's brother, who emigrated from Israel, just like us, in 1985. The latter's reasons for leaving Israel were indeed economic, and even though he was a Zionist who did his share in the battles of Israel, the bitter reality into which he was hurled broke him and forced him to do what he did. Later when I met him in New York and raised with him the question: "Why did you leave Israel?" he conceded defensively, "Listen; 15 million Jews live in this world and only 4 million of them live in Israel, and since the latter are all a minority of idiots I do not choose to belong with them." It was a painful answer that broke my heart for a while.

Obviously, I disagree with my uncle very strongly. If indeed there are idiots in this picture, they are not the people or the emigrants themselves, but rather those people who operate the governmental bureaucracy in Israel.

For years the Israeli government neglected the emigration phenomenon and avoided giving answers and solutions to soldiers who had just ended their mandatory military service, university graduates, and highly professional and skilled Israelis who could not establish and develop themselves. It passively ignored it when other countries recruited them for their services and mental capacities, and when it was required to confront the problem it went looking for the easy way of isolating the emigrants with the famous cry "a fallout of cowards." The clear purpose of the government was to release itself from blame and stigmatize the emigrants as a bunch of failures and even deserters, I might say. But the larger the number of Israelis emigrating from the country grew, the more Israel's purpose in existing was undermined. Yerida did not remain a shame anymore; rather, it became a norm. Now the Israeli society takes this phenomenon for granted, and so their own self-denial goes on.

In the United States lives the biggest Israeli community outside of Israel. I have become a witness to its successful integration into American society, together with its continuing growth. In every respectable American company, financial organization, and research institution we find Israelis. Hebrew radio and cable television programs, Hebrew newspapers, Hebrew youth movements, and Hebrew schools and kindergartens are proof that these Israelis harbor no intentions of leaving America soon. Some even brought up and gave birth to a second and third generation, who tend to further assimilate themselves into American society, a growing danger to Israel.

As long as the status quo in Israel doesn't change, the emigration phenomenon will persist, and as of now Israelis do not need to find reasons and excuses any longer in order to leave Israel; all they need is a friend or a relative who had left Israel before them, as, to my sorrow, many of them already have.

We all know the myth of the American dream and the land of unlimited opportunities. We all know the image of our nation, Israel, as the land of impossibilities and limitations. The American myth was rooted in our brains very well, thanks to those *yordim* who came once in a while for a quick homeland visit in Israel. They led us to believe that life abroad was much more comfortable and prosperous, by telling impressive stories, exaggerated and distorted but nevertheless very convincing. This is indeed the myth that persuaded my parents to go out and look for its reality, a myth that caused me, as part of a vast herd, to travel in their footsteps, a myth that dazzled thousands of young and invaluable Israelis, a myth that deprived the land of impossibilities and limitations of the opportunity to improve its image, since this myth shifted a whole generation of Israel's people from following in the steps of outstanding Zionists and pioneers.

A Fragile Alliance

As a young Israeli teenager who had relatives in America, I was enchanted with the American myth; it caused me to think about the relationship between Israel and the United States in a certain way. I imagined it was akin to special relationships such as those existing between sisters or even between a mother and her daughter. Once I even went so far as to believe that God had destined the United States of America to be the guardian angel of the young Jewish state.

After I came to America and was engulfed in the frustrating process of acclimation, through which I matured in great measure, I have learned to see the alliance between the two countries quite differently. In order to understand what I have learned, we need to understand the American mentality first.

The American mentality is like the mentality of businessmen: If they do not see any positive prospectives in their investment, they will not go for it. Their sentiments are limited to the dollar and power of maneuvers alone.

But neither the American mentality nor the Israeli mentality is a major factor in this issue, because the relationship between the two countries has always been propelled by force of mutual exploitation, which was created as a result of a global situation that affected them in similar ways. Now that this global situation has changed, apparently in a direction that provides the United States with a clear political advantage, Israel's counterbalance in this net of relationships has been compromised greatly.

Later in my analysis I came to make the following observations:

A) The American superpower has lost its economic momentum. Its giant manufacturing base gave way to the innovative thinking of its Japanese and German competitors. The quality and productivity the American labor force was known to have deteriorated as a result of social neglect and therefore contributed to economic growth unparalleled by growth in the standard of living in American society. This trend is forcing the American nation to change its approach to foreign affairs, concentrating more on domestic affairs. On the other hand, Israelis still tend to take the economic aid given to Israel by the United States for granted.

B) New generations have grown up in the two countries. In the United States a generation that did not witness the trauma of the Holocaust and World War Two has matured. They have grown into a new wave of nationalism, xenophobia, and social hatred that is expanding all over the world, while more and more American Jews are being swept by the raging stream of assimilation. This, together with the other factors mentioned, will only deepen the apathy of the United States toward Israel in the future. In Israel, on the other hand, a generation that did not witness the establishment of the state or the living conditions the pioneers endured as they worked to improve the nation of Israel for the sake of the coming generations has grown up. They enjoy a standard of living that was mostly made possible due to foreign aid, by the United States especially. They did not learn to follow in the exalted ways of their Zionist fathers and cre-

ated an image of themselves as spoiled and materialistic people, an image that only adds to the revulsion
that other nations hold for them.

C) The obsession of Israel with the American dollar and
the American obsession with power to dominate and
control have enslaved the Israeli economy at the
hands of American politics. It seems that Israeli governments have become puppets of American presidents.

Israel has never been blinder to its economic dependence. She refuses stubbornly to confront the gloomy reality
and thus ask to terminate her dependence. If she will not
wake up, and fast, before the imminent disaster, than I cyni-
cally wish for my people that one day they will wake up to
learn that the American valve has been shut off, in hope that
the magnitude of the shock will teach them the necessary
lesson.

A Hostile Minority

What concerns me more than anything else with regard
to the state of Israel is the credibility of her Jewish character,
hence the legitimacy upon which she exists.

In our declaration of independence was reported on the
part of the Gentiles in building this legitimacy, and I quote:
"On November 29, 1947, the General Assembly of the United
Nations adopted a Resolution for the establishment of an
independent Jewish State in Palestine, and called upon the
inhabitants of the country to take such steps as necessary on
their part to put the plan into effect." And please allow me
to emphasize again: " . . . adopted a Resolution for the establishment of an independent Jewish state . . . " PERIOD!!!

In reality, the state of Israel was established to exempt

the Gentile nations of a social burden. Since no other state was willing to absorb the Holocaust refugees, because of economic and anti-Semitic reasons, that decision was inevitable.

The Jews of the land of Israel indeed took the necessary steps to carry out the Resolution, as the declaration of independence continues: "The state of Israel will be open to the immigration of Jews from all countries of their dispersion," what is known as the cornerstone to the Law of Return, only the founding fathers did not care to notice the lines that came afterward and their clear and profound contradiction:

> The state of Israel . . . will uphold the full social and political equality of all its citizens without distinction of race, creed or sex . . . we yet call upon the Arab inhabitants of the state of Israel to return to the ways of peace and play their part in the development of the state, with full and equal citizenship and due representation in all its bodies and institutions—provisional or permanent.

If, indeed, we were to be true to these words, then the Law of Return should have been repealed and declared unconstitutional a long time ago. However, our fathers knew what the fate of the Jewish state would be without it. Nevertheless, they allowed the most important political document in contemporary Jewish history to be an embodiment of hypocrisy and self-denial.

Recognizing the Arab minority of the land of Israel is an integral part of the Jewish state was to my mind self-denial, and today even more than ever for several reasons. First, the Arab residents of Israel never undertook upon themselves as a collective group to contribute to public peace and the construction of the state. First and foremost, they themselves never accepted their Israeli citizenship willingly. Many of the Arab residents of Israel today, unlike their fathers, frankly admit and in public that they are Palestinian Arabs, that they share the political aspirations of their brothers in the Occupied Territories, and that they support the PLO and Islam fundamentalism as the only entities that lead and represent them. Second, the Arabs see the Jews as occupants who stole their lands, looted their properties, and robbed them of their dignity. Hence our honest efforts to try to appease the Arab minority with economic and technological incentives and social bonuses and our willingness to help them out of their isolated and primitive lives into the mainstream of a modern Israeli society are seen by them as insulting gestures and pitiful behavior reflecting weakness and desperation on our part.

As of today the Arabs have learned that they cannot reclaim their "stolen lands" by war. They have adopted the virtues of patience, demography, and democracy as their new weapons. Together with the support of the Jewish radical left and Israeli governments, they have learned to use these weapons very effectively.

Demographically, their natural growth rate always was greater than the natural growth rate of the Israeli Jews. During the 1980s the natural growth of the Arab population in Israel was 3.5 percent greater than that of the Jews. During that decade, Israeli Arabs eligible to vote learned how smart it would be to exploit the democratic process rather than boycott it. Indeed, their presence in the Knesset grew from one representative to three.

In the elections to the Thirteenth Knesset in 1992 a record was achieved when five Arab citizens were elected to our parliament. In addition, it was the first time in the history of the state of Israel that a leftist governmental coalition was supported by them quite obviously. Hence I predict with grave concern that till the end of the present century the number of Arab Knesset members will almost double.

To the frustration of most Israeli Jews, the Arab population in Israel has with undiminished success portrayed Israel to the world as a racist society unsympathetic to human rights, while in fact it's very true and clear that they enjoy a great many privileges beyond those of Israeli Jews. For instance, every Arab citizen is exempted from military service of any kind, while their Jewish counterparts at the age of eighteen must serve in the Israeli defense forces for at least up to three years and thereafter participate in reserve duty. Arab teenagers of that same age are free to start and settle their lives. They receive a three-year advance in their academic education and in their opportunities to get a job, save money, get married, and give birth to children, thereby contributing to the growth of their community. In addition, the Israeli government provides young Arabs willing to advance their higher education with scholarships and grants.

As a minority group, Arabs receive special tax incentives. Even though they are the biggest tax evaders in the country, the government restrains itself from acting as it would if the tax evaders were Jewish, because of the fear of escalating tensions and civil disobedience of the Arab minority, therefore attracting damaging and unwanted world criticism.

If we examined the government's policy toward the Arab minority we would learn that the wish to integrate them into the pioneering movement of Israel was not fulfilled and probably never will be. In fact, never before was separation between Arabs and Jews more visible than it is today. This separation is not forced; on the contrary, it is wanted by both communities and above all it is desirable. But while the Jews distinguish themselves in the purpose of upholding the Jewish character of their state, the Arabs distinguish themselves by exploiting democracy and nature with the purpose of driving Jews out of their only national possession and in hopes of converting Israel to another Arab state to add to the many already existent.

In short, I would say with utmost honesty that I fear the intentions of these Gentiles. Aside from supporting the existing social segregation, I advocate, above all, physical segregation. I simply cannot conceive in my mind any kind of role or task that the Arab minority can undertake on itself wholeheartedly by which they will become a natural part of the state of Israel, which is legitimately and constitutionally, for the most part, a Jewish state. However, unlike some individuals of the radical Jewish right, I view as appropriate the creation of a legal basis for separating and transferring the Arab minority as a provision to the final and comprehensive solution of the Palestinian issue, as I shall elaborate in the second part of this book.

*　　*　　*

Thus far I have presented, to the best of my ability, the present situation in our country in the shortest, most interesting, and most comprehensive form. My only concern is that certain Jews will characterize my description as one-sided and exaggerated; nevertheless, I trust the Jewish people, from whom I derive my faith and hope, will be able to distinguish those few Jews who benefit and will continue to benefit, on our account, if the status quo remains. Therefore, I am sure that most of us have been affected in one way or another by the situation described in this chapter. We are determined as well that this cannot stand unchanged any longer.

Addressing the issue of change cannot be done by words alone, but it is the first necessary step in doing so. Putting the words into action is an utterly different story, especially when it involves a change that requires giving up practices that have become habits. Naturally, it is very hard for a man to change the situation he lives in, even when it is bad. The reason for this is that the idea of change itself is imputed to the implications of experiencing uncertainty about the expectations and outcomes. Still this is not enough to stop a man from initiating the change, because it is his fate to live in the constant shadow of challenge.

If, indeed, you do not wish yourselves a better and brighter future, and if, indeed, the true Jewish spirit within you has gone silent, then there is no point for you to continue to read my words; but if the contrary is true, then please place my writing under your judgment.

Before I present you with the detailed program that I advise for political, economic, and social change for Israel, I feel it necessary to expose you to more hope and then prepare you for the psychological change without which the realization of my whole idea is impossible.

Chapter Two
Breaking the Myth of the Impossibility of Change

When we see Israeli Jews coming to a certain point in their lives when they raise their hands in surrender and decide to leave the country, we understand that something is extremely wrong with the system all over.

Yerida is the sign of hopelessness; it's the perfect example of a situation in which talented people with ambitions, abilities, and potentials cannot battle the bureaucratic network their government has created for them due to the priority of protecting the interests of special groups in the Israeli society. The government's efforts have been so sophisticated that even those youngsters who were just coming out of the military still full of energy and fighting spirit within them were broken enough to say, "That is it! Enough is enough!"

This phenomenon in itself is an intimidating factor, as if one is saying to the other, "Look! If they did not succeed, then you won't either."

Therefore, does this mean that our hope for a better Israel is nothing less than an illusion? Does this mean that the Jewish state has no future.

Absolutely **NOT!!!**

For Jews to believe that way is to deny their culture and all the things their fathers lived and died for. Therefore, what can we do that we have not tried already?

Taking Responsibility

It does not matter how loudly we cry for change as long as our cries remain divided. It does not matter how concerted our efforts are as long as we look to blame others for the existing situation. If we really want to know what are the roots of all of our problems, we ought to look for them in the mirror.

Exactly! We are the roots of all of our problems, and when I say "we" I am referring to each and every one of us. In other words, even though I have strongly criticized the Israeli government and its officials, let it be clear that I do not blame them for anything.

We have to do a lot of soul-searching and, at the same time, take responsibility for our own actions. Let's remember that in spite of the limitations and difficulties existing in Israel, it is still a free country. We are the owners of our country, and we must decide how to manage this entity by appointing a board of directors that will collectively manage this entity for us. If we allow them to exceed their authority and go beyond their recognized jurisdiction and then pretend we didn't notice, then we provide them with both support and legitimacy, and when we continue to provide them with such "incentives" they will become more powerful than we are. Thus the politicians in our country are not corrupt by nature, but rather the framework we created for them was spoiled from the beginning.

Hence the blaming finger should not be pointed toward the government and the authorities, because the intrigues and divisions among the public officials are mere reflections of us. That is why the message must be conveyed to the individual, to each and every family in Israel—what comprises the whole nation. The understanding must be that in a free country the citizen is the one responsible for what happens to him in life; therefore, no one is to blame for his problems, because what one cooks for himself is what he eats. On the other hand, every one of us can provide a helping hand to the other, for it is said: "All of Israel are liable one to the other."

If we will correct our personal shortcomings and turn to solve problems confronting our families, the bridge to unite the people will be much stronger. As a unified group we will have a strong and influential voice that will break any stronghold of opposition. So in order to expose the blame hiding within us and at the same time discover the potential to fix the damage made, we ought to go back to that same mirror and look into it once again.

Looking for Encouragement

Since we cannot find integrity or a model in our public servants, for it is inconceivable that they will support changing a system that works so well for them, and since the only pioneers left are those who already have lost faith in their endeavors, for they have failed so far, it seems that what we are longing for so much is wrapped in pessimism and impotence.

I do not like the idea of Jews taking examples from Gentiles, but in this fateful case, and as Theodor Herzl asserted in my introduction, we must, because there are people and nations in this world that suffered from problems and shortcomings similar to those we face now and, contrary to people's predictions, succeeded in fixing them and as a result reached lofty achievements. Also, there are those who do not reach greatness and glory yet, but they are nearing that direction through renovating or improving their political-economic systems.

The Jewish people were not destined to trail behind

Gentile nations; they were ordained by Providence to be the moral standard-bearers of humanity. This is a responsibility that we cannot avoid; that is why our road to greatness and glory is unstoppable.

* * *

The period after World War Two was an era seen in the light of renovation and human development, an era in which new states were born and old nations reborn.

Japan. Its World War Two defeat brought about the downfall of Japanese militarism and aristocratic tyranny. Japan literally became a mound of ruins, on the brink of cultural collapse. The desolation Japan became brought it back into the previous centuries, and it seemed as if the extensive rehabilitation needed to bring it back to its prior capacity would take generations to complete.

Quite remarkably, the fresh historical lesson, together with innovative thinking and the genius unique to the Japanese people, lifted the impoverished nation to heights it had never reached before. All of this was done in only one generation, and today the Japanese are still prepared with full energy to storm the world, only this time economically rather than militarily.

The similarity between Japan and Israel is that both nations are poor ones, but rich with invaluable human resources. As long as the human potential and capacity of the Jewish people are of the finest in the world, I do not see any reason why Israel cannot be as competitive as Japan and even more so.

South Korea. Its first start as an independent state came only a few months after Israel realized her independence. Historically, the Jewish people and the Korean people have a lot in common. Both lived for hundreds of years under occupation in their own homelands; both were persecuted and massacred for things that distinguished them from others. Both the states were reborn into violent and hostile conflicts that still plague them. But the similarities end where we observe the pragmatism of the South Koreans.

During the last twenty-five years the economic growth of the Korean republic has been very impressive and remarkable. Despite the need to maintain a large army, utilizing 29 percent of South Korea's budget, this nation, one of the poorest countries in the world only few years ago, has become a progressive industrial power.

Here I see the most ideal economical model for Israel. Here is a state that succeeded in transforming itself not by miracles, but by the determination, shrewdness, and mindfulness of its people. Just like Israel, South Korea suffers from a heavy defense burden and lack of natural resources; nevertheless, its economy is doing very well. Thus let us not allow it to be said that Israel's expenditures on defense and security are the real obstacle to economic prosperity of the Jewish nation.

France. This nation is in my opinion, the model for political change required in Israel, for the political history of France is a quintessential example of our political present.

No one will doubt my saying that the fall of France in June of 1940 into the hands of Nazi Germany was the result of parliamentary impasse and a noncredible administrative system of government, which failed to prepare militarily for the inevitable attack. Like Israel of today, France back then was a multiparty democracy in which the government was one made up of coalitions, not one chosen by direct popular mandate. Also, like in our case, the dominant French party was compelled to compromise its ideals and commitments to the people in order to buy support of minority parties so it could form a government; only, according to history, for most of its term it was preoccupied settling conflicts with coalition partners and as a result neglected the interests of the French nation.

Despite the tragic fate of France during World War Two, it did not learn the lesson regarding the political reasons that brought about its fall back then. Therefore, France continued to endure the decayed political establishment until 1958, when the Algerian crisis, which I compare to our present Palestinian problem, made the idea of changing the French governmental system the only condition for union, a last-ditch effort before the outbreak of anarchy and civil war. In fact, during the time between 1944 and 1958 the French people were witness to the rise and fall of twenty-two governments, which did not survive more than seven months each, so no wonder that France was torn into pieces at that time.

The end of this chapter in French history is known very well and stands to the credit of an extraordinary man by the name of Charles de Gaulle, the father of contemporary constitutional renovation in France, the founder of the Fifth Republic. Under the 1958 constitution the president of France was provided with much more powerful authority and jurisdiction, which concentrated the rule in his hands and enabled him the freedom to choose his ministers and direct the government's policies without the direct and damaging influence of small parties.

The years since then proved, contrary to the fears of many, that the French democracy was strengthened and improved despite the president's might in the new political structure. Indeed, this success has presented France with a greater political-economic stability, apparently a very impressive achievement, considering the upheavals it frequently experienced in its past.

As for the Algerian conflict, allow me to remind my readers that its resolution was made possible due to the change, and not vice versa.

The Former Soviet Union. Who would have believed that we would ever use the word *former* in regard to the Soviet Union? I assume that even the Soviet people themselves did not believe in such a possibility in the beginning; nevertheless, this change occurred in such an overwhelming manner that a new world order was created on this earth.

America would like the rest of the world to believe that the fall of the Soviet giant stands to its credit, while the real reason was the Soviet people's facing reality in the face of circumstances. The reality was a result of man-made circumstances or, in other words, an ideological system that was systematically rooted in the minds of poor peasants and unskilled workers, a system that was destined to fail, for its conceptions were utopian and its demands based on unawareness of human nature.

Although the fall of communism was good news for the world, it was an uncomfortable, drastic, and even dangerous change for those affected by it directly. The reason for this is that the Soviet people were unprepared and untrained to handle the new reality. As a result, a power vacuum was created and therefore much greater instability in our world.

In trying to connect this example to the state of Israel, all I can say is that one day we might wake up to discover a new, unwanted, unexpected reality facing us, for we have refused to rationally and reasonably admit and recognize the imperative for a certain change, thus allowing circumstances to guide themselves.

I feel this way because to my mind the structure of Israel's economy and the ideology molding it, together with Israeli politics, create an anachronistic structure, Bolshevik, I would even say, only it carries all the disadvantages of Bolshevism and lacks its advantage of centralism.

Estonia and Latvia. In 1990 they seceded from the Soviet Union and declared their independence and political sovereignty. After so many years of integration with the Soviet republics, 61.5 percent of the Estonian population were pure Estonians and 52 percent of the Latvian population were pure Latvians.

Apparently these facts made the people aware of the danger surrounding their political identity and, as it were, were the reasons for which they disfranchised the large minorities in their country from participating in their democratic process, hence depriving them of their citizenship, even though many of them were born and grew up in Estonia or Latvia.

The world remained silent to such action because there existed an understanding of the legitimate fears of the Estonians and Latvians and that there was no other way to preserve the authentic identities and characteristics of these nations.

As for the Jewish state, the same understanding must apply. But there is no comparison between the Baltic states and Israel concerning the urgency of the matter. While the Russian minorities who were born in Estonia and Latvia aspire to take part in constructing their native land, the Arab minority born in Israel long for and even conspire to achieve, I would say, the destruction of the Jewish state where they live with undoubted freedom. Moreover, unlike those Baltic states, minorities in Israel do not comprise more than 20 percent of the population; therefore, separating the Arab minority, which constitutes 17 percent of the Israeli population, cannot be as outrageous as the separation/segregation of 40–45 percent of the population in Estonia and Latvia.

Thereby we have the example of the social separation

we need in our state very urgently. Beyond that, we have proof that the nations of this world are hypocritical, ambiguous, and apathetic and tend to forget quickly, so they have no right of criticizing or condemning any action we take regarding this issue.

The United States. Since we Israelis are so obsessed with the American myth and image, I would suggest that we examine very carefully the mistakes of the American nation and especially attempt to learn the right lessons from its successes and achievements. Before it became a strong union, it endured twelve years of division and intrigues among its states, a weak economy, and even the danger of a coup, which, if it had happened, would have denied the world the privilege of witnessing the rise of the most stable, credible, and exemplary democracy of our times.

It is obvious to me that the turning point in American history that paved the way for the United States to greatness, power, and glory was the adoption of the 1788 Constitution. This event was a result of the American states' possessing greater powers and authorities than the federal government, which made it impossible for the federal government to solve the problems and crises that faced the Union. For example, it was not strong enough to establish a central bank system, regulate industry and commerce, enforce international treaties, or mobilize military force when needed.

These weaknesses affected many Americans in that age, like those who dealt in manufacturing and commerce and those who went to settle in the West without the government's protection from attacks by Indians and Spaniards. These problems and their implications brought the American people together to agree on fundamental changes needed in the Articles of Confederation and their political system. This agreement was accepted in 1787 at the Constitutional Convention in Philadelphia, at which was written the outstand-

31

ing and extraordinary Constitution of the United States of America.

But perhaps what is much more important for me to present to you is an American change of a different kind, which occurred not long ago.

While I was honored to follow the presidential election of 1992, I indeed learned that this particular democratic process is unlike any other in the world. On the one hand, I learned that the American people could not be taken for granted, as shown in the campaign of the president, George Bush, who represented twelve continuous years of Republican domination of the White House, twelve years of growing national debt and federal deficit, and four years focused on designing a new world order and solving problems of foreign nations, not those urgent ones facing America itself. On the other hand, I learned that the American people did not agree on politics as usual and instead of relying on a conventional election campaign, with one Republican candidate and the other Democratic, a third, independent candidate was called into the race. Although he was not someone very well known to the majority of people he was accepted with a surprisingly large fondness and sympathy, largely because he wasn't part of the political establishment. This candidate was the billionaire businessman Ross Perot, who reminded everyone that government is for the people and in their control, and not vice versa.

Eventually the winner was the Democratic candidate—Bill Clinton. As a young, fresh, and ambitious candidate, he reminded many of the popular John F. Kennedy; unlike past presidents, Clinton is the first one to belong to the post–World War Two generation. Finally, he was the preferred choice of the three even though he was suspected of adultery and dodging the draft during the war in Vietnam.

The reasons for Clinton's election were the American

people's need for a new beginning and repulsion toward the status quo of congressional impasse and politicians who blamed others and didn't present leadership and responsibility. Indeed, the results of the 1992 presidential elections were more a reflection of desire for change rather than the winner himself. Although everyone will have to wait in order to see whether the new president will succeed in realizing the change he promised, there is no doubt in my mind that 1992 will be registered in American history as a year of change. The reason for that is psychological.

It seems that only the coming days will tell whether the tangible change will occur; nevertheless, the real change that occurred was the one in the minds of the American people. It was reflected in the last election with the highest percentage of voters turnout in decades. Above all it was reflected in the honorable and exalted way the election campaign was ended when the losing candidates, Pres. George Bush and Ross Perot, blessed the winner, Bill Clinton, offered their help in the transition period, and urged their supporters to get together behind the new president and contribute toward healing and uniting the nation.

Like the United States, Israel will need, first and foremost, a psychological change in order to heal and renovate herself. The sons of the Jewish people in Israel will need a change in their attitude, spirit, and mind; they will need to see political opponents bridge their differences and provide priority, as always they should, to the national interests and not their own. This is perhaps the most difficult change of all, because we have been led to believe that the state of Israel cannot be changed or improved. However, this belief is fragile and could be broken very quickly. Indeed, it is something very possible just like the rest of the historical changes I have presented in this chapter were previously.

Chapter Three
The Change Is Near

The change in Israel is closer than ever. Apparently, the psychological change is even under way, as we witness the people organizing to reform the government and the political parties.

In 1992 the Labor party adopted the primary system and was the first political party to choose its candidates more honestly and directly than in the past. In contrary, it took the Likud party's losing the elections to the Knesset and government to make them understand that they, too, will have to walk according to the Labor party example, in hope that new leaders will emerge from their ranks. Also that year, Israel's Knesset "agreed" to compromise with its voters and passed the initiative binding them to change the electoral system according to which in 1996 the prime minister will be elected by universal direct mandate.

Well, the journey has begun and there is still plenty to do. We probably will have to adjust and fix the change itself as we will experience and learn more and more along the way, deciding whether the change will be what I advise or something different altogether. In addition, we will confront obstacles, especially selfish and fainthearted people who will ask a thousand questions and will give a thousand negative reasons against change in opposition to every positive reason for it. But as God is my witness, who knows better than us about the ordeals we endured across the generations? Who knows better than our enemies and foes how strong and determined we are, how unbreakable we can be?

Hence I urge all of you, dear brothers and sisters, to be brave and strong. Where you will find the will you will find the way, and those who reach the journey's end will be the brave ones who never stop marching. In short, in the light of the prophecies of our prophets we will ascend onto the king's road, the heavenly road; there we will find our salvation. Amen!

Part II

Inauguration of the Third House

Chapter Four

Not a Simple
Change—Reconstruction

In hopes that I have already laid down all the clues, reasons, explanations, and backgrounds to the concepts I am about to present as the main idea of this manifesto, this certainly is the right moment for me to roll up my sleeves and get down to the heart of the matter.

The concepts I am about to present are very real and indeed exist, but although we can be witness to and even grasp in our hands the tangible components that will be drafted here, at least a few of them will be presented in such a way that never has been conceived in our minds. In fact, these steps are revolutionary, for to execute them will require the abolition and reconstruction of specific features the state of Israel was born with and generations of Israelis grew up with.

Henceforth let it be clear that I do not intend to argue about the ideas and assertions to come later—they are my solid and well-calculated conclusion. Nevertheless, I demand of you not to discriminate or prejudge me herewith because you find the idea I advocate is irrelevant to my thoughtful approach; it deserves in its entirety your utmost attention and careful analysis, for only then will your final decision be just, fair, and complete.

Thus, according to the fundamental change that I call for, I wish to reach the following goals, which are listed according to their priority in the overall agenda:

- Clarifying and redefining the identity and relationship between the Jewish people and the land of Israel.

- Reclaiming Jewish sovereignty in their land and stressing the fact of a Jewish state in the land of Israel.
- The revival of spiritual Zionist-Hebraic values.
- Removing the impasse in Israel's government and Knesset by establishing a stable political structure.
- Fixing the economic structure in Israel and transforming it into a free-market economy.
- Achieving economic independence.
- Solving the Palestinian problem.

To my mind, these goals can be achieved by undertaking the following main actions:

- Ordaining a constitution for the state of Israel.
- Establishing a Jewish presidential democracy that will include local representation in the Knesset and separation of powers.
- Dismantling legal monopolies where necessary and proper, especially the general workers' union, the Histadrot.

In short, what I have presented here is not mere change, but a basic and complex change in the composition of the state of Israel, which will be explained in chapters to come.

Chapter Five
Solving the Palestinian Problem

I am very aware of the fact that if I address this subject first, then it will be in contrast with the priorities that were indicated before. Nevertheless, I will allow this contrast to arise, for a simple reason. Inasmuch as the people of Israel have concentrated on this problem, thus causing it to be overemphasized above much more urgent and severe domestic problems, I feel it necessary to remedy their fears and anxieties about this issue by revealing my opinion right now. However, it also is necessary to say that the required change in the policies and customs of the Israeli leadership in order for them to find a permanent, stable, and fair solution to the conflict will be made possible, in my opinion, only after the application of the scenario expressed in its total manifestation.

It will not be at all easy to realize the basic change in Israel evoked here without settling the Israeli-Arab conflict first. On the other hand, it will be almost impossible to solve this in the first place, considering the social, economic, and political status quo rooted in Israel. Under the status quo, Israel is too weak to make peace with her enemies under their current demands. They are very well aware of the paralysis possessing us; therefore, they will agree to exploit this opportunity by making peace with the intention of materializing their true sinister aspirations.

For sake of analogy I would say that our situation is similar to that which commanded France during the Algerian conflict of the 1950s. It paralyzed the French nation as a result of deep divisions between left and right, an unstable coalition, and a very fragile political structure that almost set the fire of civil war.

I hope we will not have to go that far in order to understand, as France did, that only by specific and necessary change will we be able to solve the Palestinian problem, together with other problems pursuing us.

The problem relates to two peoples who claim their right, and their right only, to live on the same piece of land. Today we all know that this problem has developed through the years into a large, violent, and very bloody conflict, it has accompanied Israel since her establishment, and it is one of the biggest challenges to counterbalance her Jewish identity, thereby endangering the final realization of the Zionist dream. Hence to my mind, an integral part of Israel's future and destiny would be settling the conflict and solving its central question—the Palestinian problem. For me it is very obvious that this understanding must not be one-sided. All parties to the conflict must know that the solution is inseparable from their natural right to live and exist within their own nations and borders; if they do not understand that, they certainly will be doomed to destroy one another.

Thus it is very important for me to point out that this chapter does not unfold a detailed suggestion of mine for solving the conflict, because, first, I am not inventing something that was not suggested before and, furthermore, I would need to dedicate all of this book to this particular subject, which is very complex and even confuses people whose wisdom and knowledge surpass mine by far.

In my search for solutions to the issue I came across opinions from all sides of the barricade, each of which was as convincing as the opposing views. Many times I adopted ideas not typical of me and yet changed them again, but when I reached closed circles of thoughts I discovered that I tend to stick to nationalistic, ideological, and uncompromising positions. Nevertheless, historical lessons and reality itself were moving forces behind the process of reaching conclusions.

Thus I have made three immediate observations:

A) Israel's political weakness does not result from the fact that she occupies Arab territories, but rather because of pitiful economic dependence on foreign aid and donations of generous but naive Jews.

B) The occupation of Arab territories and attempted control of the Arab population are only increasing Israel's economic dependence and speeding up the decay of an obsolete economic system.

C) So far Israel has avoided making a clear and final decision about the future of the Occupied Territories and the Palestinian question. Her ability to maintain such a policy as indicated by the slogan "sit and don't do" was made possible thanks to the perception that the United States would continue to foot the heavy cost of occupation and provide Israel with political and financial backing against world criticism. But unexpected events and upheavals that occurred all over the world, like, for instance, the downfall of the superpower enemy to the United States, none other than the Soviet Union, presented us with a change in the foreign policy of our old friend. This change happened in part as a result of domestic social-economic problems that were neglected by the U.S. administration during the cold war era.

My conclusions are:

A) The last perception, that Israel can trust the U.S. to keep up their economic aid, is narrow-minded and dangerous. It would only lead to increased criticism and isolation of Israel from the rest of the world. As a result, the economic neglect in Israel would deteriorate into an unprecedented catastrophe and Jewish emigration from the Jewish state would increase. In short, a demographic revolution would occur that would trample the Zionist idea that was aspired to for so many generations, and lead a whole nation onto the road of self-destruction.

B) Hence we, the Jewish people as a whole, are obligated to face the gloomy and inevitable reality and at the same time establish a revolutionary change in the way we see ourselves and the Gentiles around us.

The way we see ourselves is to be our determination only! The way we see everybody else around us is not so at all! The Gentiles around us as people and individuals are existing facts that cannot be changed by a human factor. The people of Israel, which is a union of Jewish individuals, know and understand these facts, even though this is not recognized by others. Nevertheless, just as we cannot deny and disown the Gentiles around us, they cannot do this to us either. We have proven so! We were promised so!

Going into specifics, I would point out the turning point in the Israeli-Arab conflict, the ninth of December 1987, the day when the Intifada ("uprising") broke out in protest of the Jewish subjugation of a nationalistic and proud Arab population. These days the Palestinian question has ascended to the center stage of a dramatic nationalistic conflict that had been unfolding for centuries. This was made possible because of our own self-denial, the kind that can undermine a people's existence.

I remember very well the times when I dreamed of the greater land of Israel, when I believed that a tough Jewish presence in Judaea and Samaria and on the Gaza Strip would force the Palestinians to abandon the territories, but then I remember the true bitter reality, the eclipse of the Israeli culture, values, and economy, the cohesion of Israeli Arabs and their rising power in the Israeli Knesset, the staggering growth of the Arab population compared to the Jewish population in the land of Israel, and, finally, instead of Palestinian emigration, the opposite result: emigration by many Israeli Jews, poor and rich, young and old, families and individuals—in short, a Jewish Yerida of a kind never seen since the biblical immigration to Egypt.

This reality is a direct result of the occupation and, in fact, today still portrays our people's self-denial toward the land of Israel, toward our national home, which we still dream of achieving. This evil phenomenon, like the Korah congregation, appears again and again across our generations. Like the self-hating Jews who, during the War of [Existence]/Independence of the Jewish state in 1948, followed frightened Arabs who ran for their lives fearing the vengeance of Israel's God for the atrocities they had committed against the Jews and called these Arabs to return to the villages and lands their ancestors had looted from our fathers and even urged them with pathetic supplications to give a hand to rebuilding the Jewish homeland as equal citizens while naturally no basis for, legitimacy, or even mutual interest in equality existed in the first place. Like those no less hypocritical Jews who during the 1967 Six-Day War violated the sanctity of Israel by repeating that same tragic and multicalamitous mistake. And like those Jews of our days who call themselves without shame Zionists, seekers of peace and social justice, the faithful of the leftist bloc, devotees to "the movement for inclusive Jewish renovation and assimilation," who still call for peaceful Jewish-Arab coexistence upon a land that was promised and fostered for one nation only.

As far as I can see, the state of Israel that was destined to reunite and redeem the Jewish people never materialized, and was never promised in the declaration of independence. On the contrary, the Israeli state that indeed was established in 1948 was a utopian cornerstone for a confederation between two peoples who have been deeply divided ideologically since the history of mankind was first written.

Perhaps I have exaggerated in describing the situation. After all, as of today there exists an 80 percent Jewish majority in the state of Israel. However, my exaggeration is not a cry over spilt milk, but a cry imputing a perception that is held by many in Israel who delude themselves into believing that the demographical facts will be preserved, if not improved. Therefore, they say with serenity and narrow-mindedness, "Everything will be all right."

No! Absolutely not, I say! Everything will not be all right unless the Jewish majority in Israel is guaranteed to be almost absolute, for only then will we be able to call Israel, with both confidence and certainty, a true Jewish state.

To do so will require, as I have said before, that we " . . . establish a revolutionary change in the way we see ourselves and the Gentiles around us. . . . " In other words, to do so will require an unprecedented constitutional change in Israel's political structure and at the same time unequivocal recognition of the right to self-determination of the Palestinian refugees and the Palestinian citizens of Israel.

Due to profound and long analysis of the issue, I have come slowly and reluctantly to crystallize some of the following conclusions, opinions, and positions:

A) The people of Israel must stop seeing themselves as the popular and eternal scapegoats of humanity.

They ought to stop searching after a lost justice that isn't within the reach of mortals.

B) Our past is for a reminder and lesson only, not our obsession in the present and future.

C) The Arabs of the Occupied Territories and even the Arabs of Israel are the sons of the Palestinian people. We as a nation ought to recognize this existing fact, for anything less than that will be an insult to their mentality and a time bomb ready to wipe out what we have inherited and achieved so far.

D) The state of Israel must insist on a peace initiative based on the following formula: territories and exchange of population for peace. This initiative will lead to the creation of a Palestinian state bound to territorial compromise in Judaea and Samaria and on the Gaza Strip.

E) Jerusalem is the eternal capital of Israel. She will remain undivided under Jewish sovereignty, despite any outside peace talks and negotiations.

F) The most paramount and essential provision to any agreement binding the establishment of a Palestinian state would be the recognition that the state of Israel as a result will become legally and officially what she should have become in 1948, that is, a Jewish state, a state where only Jews are privileged to be citizens, with the exception of non-Jewish residents who wish to live their lives in peace and harmony side by side with the Jews and without trying to undermine Jewish sovereignty over the land.

G) Hence all the Arabs of Israel who do not meet this provision will be deprived of their citizenship; they will be allowed to remain in Israel either as permanent or temporary residents whose natural rights, but not political rights, will be guarded by the Israeli constitution.

H) Temporary Arab residents of Israel will be required to immigrate into the Palestinian state. Respectively, all Jewish settlers in the Occupied Territories, which will be returned to the Palestinians for the purpose of creating a Palestinian state, will be required, without exception, to immigrate into the Jewish state.

I) A special commission should be appointed to coordinate reparations and resources involving the exchange of population; it should be manned by Israeli and Palestinian representatives and by American mediators.

J) It also will be very important to solve the Israeli-Syrian conflict, but absolutely not before the settlement with the Palestinians. The Golan Heights, which are an important factor in the dispute, unlike the rest of the Occupied Territories are not implicated with the problem of the subjugated Arab population, and therefore I believe that Syria could be compelled to sign a peace for peace treaty without Israel's relinquishing the Golan Heights to its control.

The opinions manifested hereby, aside from being my wishes, are rational possibilities that under the prevailing reality and circumstances are second to none; they hold the moral and just solution to the problem. In case peace does not prevail between Israel and Palestine even after such an agreement has been signed, I still would not regret my position, for I prefer a pure Jewish country in a state of war with her neighbors to a Jewish country with a large, hostile, and malignant Arab minority that enjoys peace with her neighbors.

In summary, it is obvious to me that here, just like with

the things I have said so far, my opinion will not be accepted by many Jews and especially Arabs. Therefore, the only option left would be war. To my regret, war can be utilized to provide Israel with a powerful and destructive counter-balance. However, this is not enough to assure constant victory or a solution to the problem, and as I said in the beginning of this chapter: "All parties to the conflict must know that the solution is inseparable from their natural right to exist within their own nations and borders; if they do not understand that, they certainly will be doomed to destroy one another."

Chapter Six
A New Theory of Government for Israel

From the moment a government becomes unaccountable to the people, the latter reserve their natural right to rise up and change it. Apparently, lack of communication and accountability is the reason for the high tide of voices demanding reform and change in the Israeli government and its structure.

The people of Israel are in a desperate situation. Their government is deeply divided between secular and religious forces and between the radical left and the radical right. The country is coming apart at the seams; the herd is scattering all over and getting lost. Such a situation calls for the action of a shepherd, in our case a dominant leader superior to the political establishment by virtue of distinction, who will be directly accountable to the people and will be able to channel between the divisions and bridge the differences.

The effectiveness of a government, in my view, is at its best when the government is most centralized, a centralism supported by popular will and mandate and not by dictatorial decree. But there will be those who say that centralism in any case means oppression and tyranny—a potential combination of which I am very aware. On the other hand, centralism is just another manifestation of democracy.

In parliamentary democracy for example, like the one we practice right now, the popular mandate is vested in and shared between the political parties. On the other hand, in a presidential democracy, where the political parties also play an undiminished role, the popular mandate after all is vested in and centralized in the hands of one man who is the president. Therefore, I hold the presidential system both as a political form of centralism and a form of democracy appropriate for the honor and respect aspired to by our people.

Still, lacking any experience with the suggested scenario raises again our fears of a situation in which one person will succeed in deceiving the naive majority and force his decrees against the will of many. Well, at least we are smart enough to know that no political system in past or present was perfect in the sense that it could prevent coup attempts. In fact, history has taught us that necessarily, and especially, from the various democracies that have existed have ascended some of the cruelest and most sinister dictatorships ever known. Hence if the stability of a political system, and democracy especially, is pending upon the untainted virtues and life-styles of the Jewish people, then the future of democracy in Israel is safe. However, overconfidence is liable to be deceptive; therefore, we should not underestimate the necessity of taking precautions.

I hold separation of powers and the mechanism of checks and balances as the best precautions and the most effective shields against tyranny. The United States is the best proof of that, but since there cannot be a comparison of the needs and customs of the Israeli people with those of the American people, please allow me to suggest the following model of government. The new governmental system in Israel should consist of components of the American and French system, in addition to Israeli improvisations relating to concepts that are established in our current political system and are good in nature; thereby, using them will enable the Israeli people to acknowledge the entire composition with more ease.

Cleaner Politics

Before we even start discussing a new political system we must uproot an old political practice, because it might very well contaminate its successor, thereby making it just as useless as its predecessor.

In Israel today there are no strict controls over political contributions, no prohibition of political contributions from abroad, and no specific regulations to restrict amounts of contributions. These loopholes have subjected Israeli politics to "prostitution" in broad daylight. Ironically, there have been several situations in which political parties in Israel knowingly and unknowingly receive contributions from the PLO, Saudi Arabia, and other enemy and terrorist sources. Not only is this outrageous, but in my view it is high treason.

A second example of such lust and corruption was revealed very clearly this year when the state controller report came out. It reported on contributors who gave huge sums of money to more than one political party. In another section of the report the state controller accused the Labor party of buying its way to power in the 1992 elections by paying off Knesset members who supported the no-confidence vote in the previous government and, in one particular case, paying a bribe to a small religious party so it wouldn't participate in the elections to the Histadrot of 1989.

These and many more examples reveal what kind of government and politicians we are voting for. Such practices must be stopped. First, political contributions from abroad must be prohibited; otherwise we will allow foreign interference in our domestic affairs and our sovereignty as well. Second, we must legislate specific laws to limit and cut the amount that can be contributed to a political party. Last but not least, a specific code should be written to point out the do's and don'ts during a political campaign.

Separation of Powers

The new Israeli system of government will consist of:

A) *The president of the state of Israel,* who will be elected for a term of five years by a direct popular mandate.
B) *The Knesset,* whose members will be elected for a term of four years by regional and collective elections in order to put the political parties as a counterbalance to the direct election of the president by the naive majority.
C) *The High Court of Justice,* which will be appointed by the president but confirmed by the Knesset only.

As for the mechanism according to which the new government will operate, in addition to other details that would help sustain the national integrity, I call for ordaining a constitution for the state of Israel.

A Constitution

As a Jew, I know that the supreme law standing before us is the one given to us by God on Mount Sinai. However, after many years of exile and assimilation, the Jewish people were distanced from their God. When they returned to their historical homeland and started establishing themselves as independent people once again, the removal from God became even greater as a result of political religious compulsion by a Hasidic minority over a secular majority. Hence the pure and beautiful Jewish religion has become a victim of politicization, which has made it repulsive and undesirable.

Although I associate myself with the secular majority in Israel, I hold high regard for my religion. I have my faith in it, and I truly believe in the approaching coming of the

Messiah. But under the present circumstances I see it is necessary to ordain a constitution for the state of Israel written by man, a constitution that will help secular Jews by restraining the involvement of Judaism in Israeli politics, a constitution that will enable us as a nation to bridge the gap between us and God by making the constitution a tool that will help us get back the discipline, values, and unity that our people are so well known for. And in hopes that we will be worthy of the coming of the Messiah, it will be indicated in the constitution about its own termination when the longed-for prophecy comes true.

Another reason I strongly advocate a written Israeli constitution over the unwritten one we already have is the sad fact that Jews, and Israeli Jews in particular, do not know how to respect and honor unwritten rules. Even God in His own power and glory recognized this shortcoming of His chosen ones, and due to His knowledge of our will to maintain the covenant with Him and our need for His guidance and instruction, He gave us the written law, the Torah, which has sustained us with honor and glory in the face of the dangers and misfortunes we endured.

Thus, in my opinion, the constitution of the Jewish state ought to be as clear, straight to the point, inclusive, and moderately flexible as possible and, especially, as short as possible.

Chapter Seven
Outlines to the Constitution of the State of Israel

Preamble

In our quest for the political theory that will stand before us as an indicator of the moral and untainted governmental composition of the Jewish nation and that will help us, with the light of the visions of the prophets of Israel, to build a loftier future for our posterity, we hereby find, establish, ordain, and declare the constitution of the state of Israel.

A Jewish Democracy and Its Government

A) The state of Israel is a cohesive and independent Zionist democracy whose national sovereignty belongs to and resides with the Jewish people, who exercise and express it by representation and referendum.

B) The state of Israel will be based on separation of powers, her government composed of a president, the Knesset, and the High Court of Justice.

Human Rights

The state of Israel will not deprive any man of his rights to life and liberty, peace and security, property, welfare, and happiness, and freedom of worship, conscience, language, education, and culture, which are natural and insurmountable rights given to him by the Creator, Almighty God.

The Right to Privacy, Speech, Assembly, and Justice

Except in times of war, rebellion, public danger, or danger to the Jewish democracy and people, the state of Israel will not deprive any man of his right to privacy, expression, and association in a political organization or peaceful assembly. She will not punish or imprison him for any crime without giving him an appropriate and fair trial in a court of law and justice. He will not be forced to testify against himself, nor will he be tried twice for the same crime; his property will not be confiscated for public use without fair compensation.

Citizenship

A) All members of the Jewish nation, without exception and without considering their origin, life-style, or religious conceptions, are entitled to automatic citizenship in the state of Israel. Jews who were born and live in the diaspora are invited to immigrate and settle in Israel, therewith redeeming their citizenship.

B) All who are born abroad to parents who both are Israeli citizens are automatically Israeli citizens too.

C) Non-Jews who are not of Arab origin and who were Israeli citizens before the establishment of this constitution will retain their full citizenship on the basis of appropriate political and social justice and can bequeath this privilege to their sons and daughters only.

D) In face of self-evident circumstances, all Arab citizens of Israel will be totally disenfranchised of their citizenship and political rights, and with respect to security considerations of the state and the Jewish people only a limited number of Arabs will be provided permanent residence. If a permanent resident leaves the state's boundaries for a continuous period of a year or longer, this permanent resident status will be terminated. All the rest will be provided with temporary residence status until the finding of and agreement on a permanent solution to the Palestinian question. If a temporary resident leaves the state's boundaries before such an agreement is made for a continuous period of a year or longer, his temporary resident status will be terminated and he will not be allowed to return for any reason whatsoever.

E) Israeli citizenship will not be given to persons who are born in Israel to non-Jewish parents who are not citizens of Israel.

F) Israeli citizenship will not be given to non-Jews who marry Israeli citizens and aren't Israeli citizens themselves.

Rights and Duties of Residents

A) The state of Israel will guarantee the natural and basic rights of her permanent and temporary residents. She will guarantee and be responsible for their safety and welfare, providing that in return they respect Jewish sovereignty and honor the rights of all to peace and tranquillity within the state's boundaries.

B) These obligations towards the temporary residents will cease from the moment a permanent solution and agreement is found regarding the Palestine question.

The Right to Vote

A) The right to vote in the state of Israel will be the exclusive possession, with no exceptions, of every citizen who is eighteen years old or older.

B) The state of Israel will enact the proper laws and means in order to assure the right to vote of the sick and disabled and will provide proper arrangements for absentee voters who wish to exercise their right.

C) Israeli citizens whose permanent residence is outside of Israel will participate in the presidential elections only.

D) All eligible voters will vote for only one electorial district in the elections for the Knesset. The electoral district they will vote for will be determined according to their official and permanent residence in Israel.

The Knesset—the Legislative Branch

A) All legislative powers and jurisdictions provided herein will be vested in the Knesset of Israel. It will consist of 120 representatives who will be elected for a term of four years in universal, confidential, collective regional elections.

B) The state of Israel will be divided into twelve electoral districts as equal in population as possible, and every consecutive four years from the moment of establishing this constitution the state will conduct a census in order to maintain this partition accordingly.

C) Elections to the Knesset will take place simultaneously in all electoral districts. Every district will have ten representatives in the Knesset; they will be elected in proportion to mandates received by their political party.

D) The Knesset will decree the appointed times and places where elections will be held for the Knesset and presidency. But in case the Knesset votes no confidence in the president or the latter submits his resignation to the chairman of the Knesset, new elections for both the Knesset and presidency will be called no later than sixty days from the moment the no-confidence motion is passed or the president's resignation is accepted.

E) No person shall serve in the Knesset before he reaches the age of twenty-one and no person shall serve who did not perform his duty in the Israeli defense forces or in any other national service. He will be an Israeli citizen and resident for at least five years of the electoral district he intends to represent.

F) In case any vacancy occurs in the Knesset, the political party to whom the vacant seat is mandated will appoint a substitute, providing he meets the above qualifications.

G) The Knesset will chose its officers and chairman providing that the latter is a Jewish citizen, determine its own rules of conduct and establish regulations and procedures to arrange the agenda, judge the integrity and qualifications of its members, and, with the agreement of eighty members, expel or disqualify a member.

H) A majority of one hundred members will constitute a quorum to pass a motion and administer the order of the day. If a quorum is not achieved, the members present are allowed to hold discussions and debates and punish or fine the absentees according to rules the Knesset will formulate.

I) The Knesset will maintain a book of chronicles, wherein will be recorded all discussions and debates during Knesset meetings. From time to time it will publish the above, in addition to the names of those voting "yea" and "nay" for various motions and the veto or approval by the president of the various motions. Discussion regarding the security of the state that involves secret information will not be published.

J) Every motion to pass three readings will be presented before the president. If he signs it, then the motion will become a law, but if not, the motion, together with the objection, will be returned to the Knesset, which will reconsider the motion. If the motion is then passed by a majority of eighty members then it will become a law.

K) All sections, provisions, and clauses to constitute a motion ought to relate to the original issue and purpose for which the motion was initiated.

L) The Knesset will determine the amount of compensation given to all civil servants, including judges, the president, ministers, and themselves. All motions initiating increase in compensation will be passed in the following manner:

First reading—simple majority
Second reading—majority of seventy members
Third reading—majority of eighty members

Any increase in compensation will come into effect with the start of the following term of the Knesset.

M) All motions involving religious matters will be passed by three readings similar to those indicated in the clause above.

N) Knesset members will not serve during their term in office in any other public or private office. They cannot resign for the purpose of serving in another public office that was established during their term in the Knesset.

O) All Knesset members are bowed and equal before the law.

P) The Knesset will hold the power and jurisdiction to:

i) Levy and collect taxes, duties, impositions, and tolls that are reasonable and necessary for the security and welfare of the state of Israel.

ii) Pay the national debt and borrow money against the credit of the state of Israel.

iii) Regulate industry, commerce, banking, and public services required for the prosperity of Israel.

iv) Regulate transportation and communication.

v) Support and enable the advancement of science, technology, art, education, and culture and guarantee the rights of authors, inventors, and artists.

vi) Regulate the absorption of Jewish immigration.

vii) Ordain inferior courts to the High Court of Justice.

viii) Determine the punishments for crimes committed against the public and the state and for all hate crimes and atrocities committed against the Jewish people in their homeland or abroad.

ix) Fund and support the Israeli defense forces and police and establish any defensive force necessary and proper for the security of the state and Jewish people.

x) Pass state-of-emergency powers to the president, providing that during times of war, rebellion, or civil unrest there exists, in the judgment of the Knesset, danger to the public or to the Jewish democracy and people.

xi) Pass all laws that are necessary and proper in helping to carry out all the mentioned powers, duties, and responsibilities that this constitution provides and/or does not prohibit.

The President—the Executive Branch

A) All executive powers and jurisdiction will be vested in the president of the state of Israel, who will be elected for a term of five years in national, universal, confidential, and direct elections.

B) Every political party or petition of at least 100,000 eligible voters can nominate a candidate for the presidency.

C) No person who has not been a Jewish citizen at least ten years and who did not serve in the Israeli defense forces or any other national service shall become president before or after the age of thirty.

D) The candidate to become president, provided that he meets the qualifications above, will be the one who wins the majority of votes. If no candidate receives the required majority, a second round will be held no later than seven days after the first round. The second round will be held between the two candidates who received most of the votes in round one. The candidate to win most of the votes in round two will become the president of the state of Israel.

E) The president will make the sole and exclusive decisions in appointing his government's ministers and officers; he'll be able to discharge anyone in his government and replace them as well.

The president will nominate a vice president and judges with the advice and consent of the Knesset.

G) No member of the legislative or judicial branch will serve in the president's cabinet.

H) The Knesset can discharge a minister in the presidential government by a majority vote of eighty Knesset members.

I) The Knesset can vote no confidence in the president and his government by a majority vote of ninety Knesset members. In such case the president and Knesset will continue their services temporarily until a new president and Knesset will be elected within a period no later than sixty days from the moment no confidence was voted.

J) The same procedure established in the clause above will apply when the president submits his resignation to the chairman of the Knesset.

K) In cases when the office of the presidency becomes vacant as a result of death or inability to carry out the duties of the president, the vice president will become the new president provided that he meets the qualifications established in item C. If he does not meet the qualifications, he will temporarily serve as president until a new president is elected, within a period of no later than sixty days from the moment the vacancy occurred.

L) The president's cabinet can initiate any kind of legislation the Knesset is authorized to pass. The president and his ministers may present and defend their motions in person at the Knesset and in return might be required to answer questions of Knesset members.

M) The president is the chief national representative of the state of Israel. He leads in matters of policy and signs agreements and treaties with nations of the world, except for peace treaties with enemy nations, which have to be approved by a Knesset majority vote of eighty members.

N) The president of Israel is the commander in chief of all Israeli defense forces and guarantees the safety of the public and the Jewish people. In times when he is given state-of-emergency powers by the Knesset, he will do all that is necessary and proper to secure the stability, independence, sovereignty, and territorial integrity of the state of Israel.

O) The president may from time to time show clemency to public offenders and on basis of good behavior give them amnesty.

P) The president, the vice president, the cabinet ministers, and all of his officers are bowed and equal before the law.

The High Court of Justice—the Judicial Branch

A) All judicial powers will be vested in the High Court of Justice and the inferior courts.

B) All judges will be appointed for life on condition of good behavior and respect for the law.

* * *

The basic idea behind the concept of the judicial branch in this constitution must be its ability to interpret the constitution and check and counterbalance the executive and legislative branches in order that they not exceed their authority and violate the constitution.

Under what is customary today, the Knesset can bypass the High Court's decisions on controversial issues by passing counterlegislation, thereby removing the restraint from itself. Thus, in order to emphasize the idea of separation of powers, we need a judicial branch that will be able to declare certain legislation or a certain presidential action unconstitutional. On the other hand, the judicial branch should not be allowed to judge the morality and constitutionality of the constitution itself but rather judge within its framework only. Third, the High Court's ruling about constitutional issues should be made only when a complaint is raised in the appropriate court.

In short, since I am no lawyer and see this particular issue is beyond my power, experience, and skill, I will leave the foundations I have drafted here to be worked out completely by the best intellectuals among us.

Limitation of Religion from State

I carefully chose to call this concept limitation and not separation of religion from state, because it would be wrong to stereotype Judaism as a religion only. Judaism is a broad spectrum of life-styles—a whole civilization by itself encompassing the Hebrew language, common historical development and background, folklore, Zionism, and, last but not least, religious beliefs, commandments, customs, and rules of conduct.

Since the major Jewish religious problem to disturb the peace and freedom of choice of Israelis is the involvement of small religious parties in Israeli politics, their disproportionate influence on domestic and foreign policy, and their tough interpretation of "who is a Jew," we must seek to eliminate this kind of religious compulsion and politicization, because it undermines and confuses our Jewish identity in general and dilutes our religion in particular.

The Israeli constitution must take a neutral position with regard to the question of whether Israel should be a secular or religious Jewish state. On the one hand, Israeli Jews must have the freedom to chose their life-styles; on the other, religion must take its place in molding a national image and unity.

Hence here is what I think the constitution should say in this regard:

A) The state of Israel shall not pass a law that will interfere with the personal right of Israeli Jews to be secular.

B) The interpretation of "who is a Jew" shall be delegated to the Orthodox, Conservative, and Reform rabbinates. In case a dispute shall arise about the Jewishness of an individual, each rabbinate shall declare its yea or nay; if two nays shall be ruled, then the individual is not a Jew, but if two yeas are ruled, then the individual is a Jew.

Ratifying Amendments

A) The president, the Knesset, or a petition of 100,000 eligible voters can initiate an amendment to the constitution, providing that the national sovereignty will always belong and reside with the Jewish people and will not be diminished as a result.

B) The process of ratifying an amendment will begin in the Knesset with the following three reading procedures:

First reading—majority of seventy members
Second reading—majority of eighty members
Third reading—majority of ninety members

Providing that the amendment passes this procedure,

it will require the final ratification of a universal, national, direct referendum; a simple majority of the people will enact and ordain the amendment as part of the constitution.

Termination of the Constitution

In hope that with the help of God this political theory, in parallel with the divine instruction that is rooted in the depths of our hearts, minds, and souls, will lead and guide us to be worthy of the coming of the Messiah, our savior, this constitution on that event will be terminated and Heaven's Kingdom will descend upon us. Amen!

*   *   *

One generation from now, the faithful of the renovated Jewish state will win the majority of seats in the Knesset as a result of a national security crisis, a deep economic recession, and political collapse as well. The nation will reach a crossroad that could lead her, on the one end, on to greatness and glory or, on the other end, on to irreversible calamity and destruction. Thereupon the plan and promise of the renovated Jewish state will be the last alternative and the only salvation; her faithful will carry it out with the people's support and mandate.

The faithful of the renovated Jewish state will establish a temporary emergency government for a period of six months in order to rescue Israel from imminent danger. After the state of emergency is over, an interim government will be formed whose task will be to prepare the nation for transition to a presidential system. Also during the period of transition, a constitution shall be written and presented for the people to decide on.

When the mandate of the interim government is over, the constitution will go into effect providing it was approved by national direct referendum. Within 60 days thereafter, Knesset and presidential elections will take place, the new government will come into being, and Israel will then truly become Israel.

Chapter Eight
An Israel That Prospers

The strength of the Israeli economy is the key to survival of the Jewish nation and, therefore, the moving force behind the Zionist idea. This understanding, I believe, is a lot easier to convey to the people, because it is self-evident and similar to the simple logic of the individual. To illustrate that, I would say that a strong Israeli economy would be a powerful force to attract Jewish immigration from Western countries, where most diaspora Jews remain living in relatively high comfort and with a high standard of living. Moreover, such a scenario might positively change Israel's counterbalance in the conflict with the Arab nations and Palestinian people, thereby providing a better opportunity for permanent and comprehensive peace and security in the Middle East.

Hence the questions that ought to be asked are:

A) Is the Israeli economy strong and stable?
B) If Israel's problem lies with her economy, why the need for the political change I advocate?

The answers are:

A) This is a rhetorical question.
B) Our political mechanism is mostly rooted in the Israeli economic structure; that is why it ought to be changed.

Nevertheless, if the coming years prove to me that our present political system is capable of dealing with the economic problems and challenges of our country, then I will utterly revoke and abandon the political idea that I have introduced. But since I do not see any possibility for political consensus in a system that cherishes multiparty government over a strong, cohesive, and responsible government, my assertions and opinions still stand.

There are not many ways to strengthen the Israeli economy!

First and foremost, we must utterly revoke and abandon the entire socialist ideology, for it is officially obsolete since the fall of the communist empire.

Second, we must open the Israeli market for accelerated privatization, investment, free but fair competition, and free enterprise.

Third, the government must limit its present involvement in the economy to a level that is no greater than is necessary and proper.

Fourth, we ought to pay our national debt as soon as possible, in order to remove our economic dependence and thus not damage our credit and good name.

I do not say that it will be easy to undertake these steps. They also will not happen quickly. It will take at least five or ten years and, who knows, maybe even a generation; nevertheless, we ought to carry them out in a collective and coordinated manner, with absolutely no delays.

A Free Market Economy

Israelis treasure within them invaluable, high-potential capabilities. However, bureaucracy and political intrigues and conspiracies have blocked their emergence and even frustrated realization of ambitions.

A strong economy relies on the impudence, boldness, shrewdness, mindfulness, and innovativeness of its people. These virtues are in no shortage among the Jewish people and, indeed, attract the jealousy of others. Therefore, in order to strengthen the Israeli economy we must give these traits the freedom of expression by undertaking the following measures:

- The only role the Histadrot should play in our economy is that of a labor union; thus it is necessary to dismantle it as it exists. First and foremost, its officers must be forbidden from serving in any public or governmental office. The government has to take over all the factories and companies of the Histadrot; it ought to sell them to private entrepreneurs, liquidate the assets of the Histadrot, and divide them accordingly among the union members.
- The government ought to discontinue legal monopolies in agriculture, communications, broadcasting, sports, air, and intercity transportation.
- The Israeli tax code has to be reviewed and rewritten from A to Z. All small tolls and impositions must be repealed; the new tax system must be centralized around the following sources of revenue: income tax, sales tax, social security tax, national health insurance tax, corporate tax, luxury tax, and gasoline tax.
- The government ought to encourage private investments and the establishment of small businesses with tax incentives and low-interest loans.
- The government should encourage big private investments from abroad by giving special tax exemptions for long but reasonable periods of time. This policy should be targeted for the rich Jewry abroad, the same who are sending donations today, because in the past their investments in Israeli factories and industry were "sabotaged" by governmental bureaucracy and Histadrot monopolization.

- The government ought to better regulate and control the procedures the banks use in order to provide credit to the public, so as to eliminate uneconomical consumption, which increases the national debt and fosters a materialistic mentality.
- The government ought to sell government-owned lands to civil and private sectors under proper and affordable terms.
- Israeli industries and companies should be encouraged to invest in new technologies and products.
- The government ought to initiate and target the research and development of future industries. It should provide grants to universities that operate research and development and it should provide tax incentives to companies that will create or invest in systems, products, and ideas that are beneficial to the welfare of the public, the state, and especially the environment.

Jewish Labor

"Jewish labor in the land of Israel" is the slogan of Zionism. In fact, it was the cornerstone to the establishment of the state of Israel. However, through the years Jewish labor was swept aside, to be replaced by cheap and unskilled Arab labor.

The generation born after 1967 was infected with the notion that hard physical work does not fit its dignity and was obsessed with luxury and squandering, infatuated by euphoria and pride. Today this mentality has become a cutting reflection of the economic reality in Israel and proof of the downfall of Zionism.

Our economy has become more and more dependent upon the Arab work force, a trend that means de facto recognition of 2 million Arabs as an integral part of the Jewish state, a trend we absolutely cannot afford.

An effective battle against unemployment and the Palestinians would be the revival of the Jewish pioneering spirit. In my opinion, if we Israelis will go back and do what the Palestinian Arabs are doing for us now then there will not be unemployment.

Here is what the government has to do:

- Establish special courses in the army that will train young volunteers in agriculture, infrastructure, and construction jobs and incorporate them in labor corps that will undertake national public projects. In return, the military duty of all volunteering soldiers will be shortened.
- Cut unemployment benefits and reorganize the system in such a manner that will force people to participate in public work.
- Open up a campaign (propaganda, if you will) through educational institutions and the press that will educate the public, including the younger generations, with work discipline and ethics.
- Limit the number of working permits issued to noncitizens and Palestinians especially.
- Establish a police authority, similar to immigration authorities in the United States, that will prevent foreigners' working illegally. An employer that is caught providing work to an illegal worker will be given heavy fines; the illegal worker, on the other hand, will be deported.

Dispersal of the Population

This issue of spreading population from dense urban

areas to unsettled areas is a national interest, but it was managed very poorly and still is.

Since dispersal of population in Israel will serve the state economically, demographically, and politically, it ought to be considered as a paramount priority.

Economically, population density in the metropolises of Tel Aviv, Haifa, and Jerusalem contributes to traffic jams, which translate into precious working hours wasted, the high number of fatal accidents, air pollution, poor sanitation, and even crime and emotional unrest. All this means a waste of money and resources.

Demographically, population density in the mentioned areas exposes other areas, like the Negev and Galilee, to desolation and illegal Arab settlement, which is dangerous for us and sinister of them.

Politically, with regard to the political system I suggested before, it would be difficult and complex to divide the state of Israel into twelve electoral districts under the existing situation.

If we are capable of understanding the significance of these problems, then we ought to agree to the following measures:

- Encouraging companies and industries located in populated areas to relocate in the Negev or Galilee or on the Golan Heights by reducing tax rates in these areas.
- Providing affordable terms for mortgages and lands to those workers and professionals that will follow after the relocating employment sources.
- Improving the road and rail infrastructure in a planned and vigorous manner.
- Renovating the public transportation system for the sake of better mobility and a cleaner environment.

Healthier Transportation

We have too many vehicles on our roads—no doubt about that! The number of car accidents is relentlessly increasing every year. Cars and gasoline are huge portions of our imports; they damage the Israeli economy and the environment. In order to reduce waste, pollution, and car accidents, we ought to encourage Israelis to use public transportation and at the same time find and develop alternative and cleaner energy sources for our vehicles.

I believe in the use of trains as a main public transportation means between Israeli cities; Israel should develop this infrastructure in a national enterprise that provides modern trains powered by electricity or another source of energy that does not pollute.

Intercity bus transportation must be deregulated and opened to private competition. However, transportation within cities should remain under municipal and local authority.

The government ought to increase the gasoline tax, with the purpose of helping to raise funds needed to develop the road and train infrastructure and perhaps even convincing people it's better to use their cars less.

Clean and Beautiful Land

We humans have become ungrateful to the Almighty Creator. We have neglected the earth that He entrusted with us, destroyed its forests, polluted its air, exploited its treasures, wiped out its living creatures, and desecrated the divine presence over it.

The Jewish people cannot exempt themselves from this; they are just as much to blame as the others.

The Zionist enterprise returned the land of Israel to the

ecological beauty it possessed during biblical times, yet it can make Israel look even better and make her show the image and impression of Biblical beauty. The righteousness and integrity of the land are binding us to this task and duty; they oblige us to be a leading example in the campaign to save the earth from ourselves.

As of today, the state of Israel has no clear or fixed policy with regard to environmental protection and energy conservation; she does not have an organized system of disposing of various wastes and barely recycles garbage that can be processed for reuse; she does not have definite and strong legislation against water and air pollution by companies and industries.

We absolutely ought to fix this injustice!

- First and foremost, the Knesset ought to legislate laws that will require the reduction or elimination of pollution and that will institute and initiate a recycling industry. I am aware of the financial risks recycling involves at first. However, in the far future, this industry will be very economical and without a doubt will become prosperous and large. Therefore, we ought to educate our children accordingly and target the fostering of this healthy behavior, as an investment in the future of our nation.
- The government ought to provide incentives and even subsidies to establish private recycling companies.
- The government ought to incorporate in the sanitation system new, modern tools and facilities to dispose of or incinerate garbage.
- The government ought to facilitate proper means to recycle sewage of agricultural and industrial needs.
- For several years we have witnessed hard and violent winters in Israel, which caused powerful floods that

resulted in heavy damages, injuries, deaths, and waste of invaluable water. Thereupon the government ought to construct an infrastructure that would control the floods and gather the water.

- We ought to expand the use of solar, wind, and hydro-electric power.
- The government ought to increase public awareness of this issue by an effective advertising and educational campaign.

Reforming Education

Education always was and always will be the cradle of our culture; our economy and identity especially are dependent upon it.

The main problem confronting our schools is safety and security, and although we are far, in this respect, from the deplorable condition of American schools, we must not wait for such deterioration to occur.

Lately, violence and vandalism in Israeli schools have increased very sharply. Personally, this concern was the main reason that I chose to attend a military high school in Israel.

Discipline of students never was so poor. Never before was it so common for students to fear going to school because of threats and intimidations by school gangs. Never before have we seen our schoolyards become scenes for drug trafficking. I am sure the increasing trends of failure and absence from school are direct results of the conditions I described just now.

I believe there is a simple solution to this particular problem—that is, the establishment of a school safety and security guarding company that is incorporated within the police department. Every school would have a fixed number of security guards who would look out for terrorist bombs and attacks but at the same time also look out to preven violence in schools, cutting from classes, and lack of disci pline in general. In short, with their help teachers will be abl to teach and students be able to learn.

A second problem I can see is the neglect by teachers anc officers in the education ministry of students who wish tc learn and study very hard but, unfortunately, face difficul ties. Such discrimination is a senseless policy that does nol serve national interests; everyone must have an equal oppor tunity. Here is what we have to do:

- Vary curricula and student choices.
- Make school days longer.
- Provide the teachers with better salaries.
- Invest in future teachers by providing qualified young Israelis with government-sponsored scholarships as incentives to go to Israeli universities and study education.
- Shorten the school week of junior and high schools to five days instead of six.
- Expand sports programs and activities.
- Concentrate on science, technology, and job training.
- Increase the inclusion of Zionism and Judaism in curricula.
- Institute the singing of the Israeli national anthem ("Hatikva"), at the opening of each school day and install an Israeli flag in each classroom.
- Build in each school a mini synagogue, in addition to providing an optional school program that would teach interested students prayer and the everyday agenda of a congregation.
- Reform our universities and expand the involvement of colleges and private academies in providing higher education.

- Repeal the Bagrot examinations as standards for admission to public universities. Instead, replace them with a single examination that would include mathematics, reading, writing, and language.

National Health Insurance

For many years most Israeli citizens enjoyed the health insurance plan of the Histadrot and the medical care of its subsidiary, Kopat Holim, which has been suffering for many years now from a growing malignant deficit of tens of millions of dollars.

Since I explained unequivocally what should be the fate of the Histradot, it should be clear that someone else will have to take care of the health insurance of the people.

I believe that the state ought to guarantee the health of its citizens, for medical care is no privilege but a basic natural right. Under no circumstances should a person be denied medical care because of his economic status, nor should he be discriminated against by a doctor. In short, medical care is not for sale, nor for dealership, nor for the purpose of making an immoral profit.

I call for the Israeli government to fix and control all prices of medical care and services, while medical care itself is provided by private medical groups that will not be paid directly by the patients but by a national health insurance fund created by government subsidies and a health insurance tax.

Defeating the Intifada

I want Israel to live in peace with her neighbors and to

carry the initiative for peace. However, in order to do that, Israel ought to be strong.

The Intifada is undermining our national security and strength. Its escalation will not bring peace. On the contrary, it will provide the Palestinians with the feeling that Israel is weakening and can be defeated; hence they will pursue violence and terrorism as means of sabotaging the ongoing peace process. We will face another War of Existence that will become our undoing.

Those who say that the problem of the Intifada has no military solution are fainthearted Jews who cannot do anything but talk nonsense. The Israeli defense forces, with proper popular and governmental support, will defeat the uprising within several days—no doubt about it.

Palestinian terrorists must be punished within the framework of the law in two ways only: deportation and capital punishment.

Mobilizing Capital

You probably all wonder how Israel possibly can afford to pay for all of these ambitious plans. Well, she absolutely has no choice! Moreover, it seems to me that Israel will not need money as much as she needs consensus, determination, will, and the patience to carry out these plans, apparently conditions that only a stable and cohesive political system can supply.

In any case, before us are several means of mobilizing capital, and we ought to utilize them all:

- Cutting down on the size of the government and bureaucracy; cutting the salaries of Knesset members, cabinet ministers, and president and government expenditures; and canceling all fringe benefits of public officials.

- Cutting subsidy programs.
- Accelerating deregulation and privatization of government and Histrodot factories.
- Encouraging world Jewry to stop donating money, and instead start investing in Israeli industries and companies.
- Encouraging the Israeli people to increase their savings by allowing personal savings accounts to be tax-free.
- Educating our children about the importance of savings for the individual and the state and enabling them to participate in this great endeavor.
- Shortening the length of reserve and military service.
- Borrowing money from the Israeli public by issuing governmental bonds.

* * *

This is it, brothers and sisters! It is all done and complete!

With this manifesto I have spoken about a gloomy reality and how it can be changed; I have spoken about hope, illumination, and salvation; I have said how things should be fixed and how they must be fixed. It is time for us to begin debating about the future of the Jewish state in Israel. Everything else is now up to you.

Afterword: A Zionist Manifesto

Every generation has a story about their heroes and villains, about the miracles and wonders they have witnessed, about the calamities and upheavals they have endured, about their hopes, aspirations, and dreams, as well as the disappointments they have found and failures they encountered. And to every generation Providence has provided leaders and prophets who announce the vision of their time.

History is teaching us that the greatest leaders and prophets of our nation have stood before crowds of ignorant, foolish people who saw them in return as the truly irregular and insane ones. As a result, their words of truth and righteousness were accepted only after the break of a fateful tragedy they had warned of or, in good cases, just moments before it was about to happen.

To the present generation of my people, I am the one to carry the warning as well as the promise, even though I do not see myself among the prophets and I am not ordained to do so as far as I know. Nevertheless, I am keeping to myself the reason for my coming forward with this manifestation.

The envisioner of the Zionist idea who preceded me was an assimilated Jew who returned to his roots, just like me, in light of a revelation. The only thing to trouble and confuse me in this comparison is the point of differences between us that are imputed to the circumstances that caused us to assimilate in the first place.

It seems that the factors of Theodor Herzl's assimilation were understandable and to a certain measure acceptable. After all, he was born in a time and era different from that which I was born in. He was born at a time when the Jewish people lived in exile, dispersed all over the world under the rule and mercy of Gentiles who, on countless occasions, persecuted them, killed them, and deprived them of means of identifying and expressing themselves.

As for me, I was born in a time and era that many of Herzl's generation did not even conceive in their wildest dreams; it is the era in which the state of Israel exists, a Jewish state that indicates that the virtue of Jews is in their nature of being uniquely different.

Therefore, how come I was assimilated not among the Gentiles, but rather among the Jews themselves?

The establishment of the Jewish state was the peak of Zionism and simultaneously, to my regret, the turning point toward downfall. I was born in Israel in a time of modernization and renaissance that passed through the Israeli land and people with an unprecedented, unexpected speed. These were positive developments that were exploited by both Israeli society and the government and as a result undermined the significance of Zionism.

In retrospect, I was a passive and unaware witness to that. I have seen the pioneering spirit habitual in the ideology of the founding father being killed by impure habits of the political parties, by increasing dependence on Arab labor, by the donations and aid from abroad spoiling the young Israeli generations who are engulfed in the phenomena of Americanization and emigration and, moreover, by the religious compulsion orchestrated by effective and well-organized political pressure by a Hasidic, anti-Zionist minority. Action that is virtual corruption, blackmail, and hypocrisy, virtual contempt for God and Judaism, which invited in the past the destruction of our temple in Jerusalem.

My emigration from Israel resulted from this impurity, which subdues my family. As a young teenager at that time, I had mixed feelings about my family decision, which eventually made what were supposed to be the best moments of my life, moments of deep depression, moments of exile, moments in a labyrinth, moments when I wanted to put an end to my agony. Today I know that this portion of my life was a period of divine testing, a period of preparation, a period inevitable and integral with my fate and destiny.

Exile was for me the biblical occasion on Mount Sinai when I redeemed my consciousness to God, found my true connection with the land of Israel, and discovered a big Torah commandment—that is, Zionism, Zionism in its entirely.

Never before has someone come forward to set the matter straight; never before were we told the true and complete meaning of Zionism. The notion always was that Zionism aspired to establish a national home for the Jewish people in the land of Israel, gathering the exiles, advancing the welfare of the people of Israel in their land. Indeed, while these aspirations are materializing even today, we ought to know that the role of Zionism is deployed in much wider dimensions.

The place and role of Zionism in our lives, culture, customs, and even religion are sacred, for it is the original covenant between us and our Creator, the Almighty God.

From the beginning it was said: "Now the Lord had said unto Abram, 'Get thee out of thy country, and from thy kindred, and from thy father's house, unto a land that I show thee'" (Gen. 12:1).With those words Zionism was established, and with Zionism Judaism began to crystallize.

Chronologically, Abraham, our patriarch, was a Zionist before he became a Jew, for he came into a covenant with God by his readiness to connect with the land God ordered him to go onto, the land of Israel. Indeed, the holy land was given to us before the Ten Commandments were, yet righteous and loyal people would say, with all due respect, that the main reason the Jewish people survived during all these centuries was the Torah and its commandments. Only my answer to that would be that even though I do not diminish my recognition of the Torah's contribution to that fact, not only did the righteousness of Jews carry them against the odds, but rather the fact that they did not give up their hopes and dreams of one day returning to Zion, did not stop longing for freedom and liberty by calling out aloud every year, "next year in Jerusalem." This was the spring of faith and belief that pushed them to want life, the convincing reason for God, despite His frustrations with us, to continue to look after us and sustain us.

Thereupon, Zionism is a big rule in the Torah, as it is written: "from Zion Torah will come," meaning that from Zionism would come the instruction that would bring Jews back to their best nature, that would make them worthy of being the chosen ones and no doubt bring the promise of salvation.

Our salvation began in 1948 indeed, but its fate lies in our hands and depends upon the deeds and actions we will do in the near future. Our Messiah has indeed arrived, but his revelation depends on the consciousness of the people of Israel to their land and themselves. However, the biggest danger facing us and these words is not from outside, but rather from within.

On the one hand, we hear the barks of leftist Jews full of self-hatred and self-denial, who come to strengthen the hands of hostile Arabs who provoke the armies of God. On the other hand, we hear the barks of anti-Zionist Jewish Hasidim who call for the destruction of Zionism and advocate blind faith. Yet and nevertheless, I rise here before you in the name of Almighty God by saying lest you should fear, for those who bring upon us the same impurity that caused us so much misery for generations by their sinister cries against the state of Israel that arose by the fury and might of God, they remain to serve Satan and to embody the Korah congregation of our time; therefore, they will not be worthy of the Messiah and salvation.

Few are those who are aware of the true and complete Zionism, few are those who truly deserve to be called Zionists. As one who would do everything in his ability to deserve to be called a Zionist, I advise to all Jews who wish, like me, to revive their Jewishness, to integrate everyone according to his ability, diligence and love of Israel and the Torah commandments, for all of these are inseparable, just as without Zionism there is no essence to Judaism, there is no salvation, and there is no Jewish people.

Hence the Jewish people ought to understand that with the establishment of the state of Israel we reached the last station in our painful wanderings, a station from where we have no other place to go, a station from where we might ascend onto the King's road or descend down the slopes of the underworld. As a state, Israel ought to accept one of two choices: first, to be a total success, first in the front rank of nations, or, second, to be an exemplar of misfortune. But absolutely, under no circumstances, can she choose the road of mediocrity.

In short, Israel cannot be Israel without greatness and glory and that is the reason we must renovate the Jewish state.